W9-AUL-340

Scott Foresman Reading

Surprise Me!

About the Cover Artist
Maryjane Begin and her family live in Providence, Rhode Island, where she teaches college students when she is not working on her own art. Many of her illustrations—even of imaginary places—show how things in Providence look.

ISBN 0-673-59675-3

Copyright © 2000 Addison-Wesley Educational Publishers Inc.

All rights reserved. Printed in the United States of America.

This publication is protected by Copyright and permission should be obtained from the publisher prior to any prohibited reproduction, storage in a retrieval system, or transmission in any form or by any means, electronic, mechanical, photocopying, recording, or otherwise. For information regarding permission, write to: Scott Foresman, 1900 East Lake Avenue, Glenview, Illinois 60025.

4 5 6 7 8 9 10-VH-06 05 04 03 02 01 00

Scott Foresman
Reading
Surprise Me!

Program Authors

Peter Afflerbach

James Beers

Camille Blachowicz

Candy Dawson Boyd

Deborah Diffily

Dolores Gaunty-Porter

Violet Harris

Donald Leu

Susan McClanahan

Dianne Monson

Bertha Pérez

Sam Sebesta

Karen Kring Wixson

Scott Foresman

Editorial Offices: Glenview, Illinois • New York, New York
Sales Offices: Reading, Massachusetts • Duluth, Georgia • Glenview, Illinois
Carrollton, Texas • Menlo Park, California

Contents

Surprise Me!

Unit 6

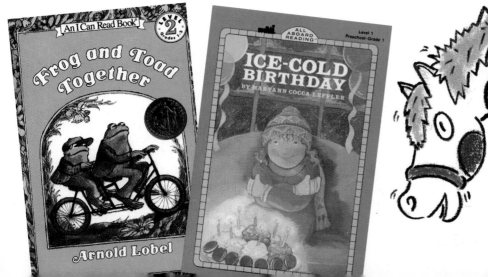

5

Surprise Me!

How do we get all those great ideas?

Bluebirds in the Garden

by Deborah Eaton
illustrated by Meg Aubrey

My name is Cheyenne. Come see my garden. It's out here, in my yard. Do you know what I'm growing? It is **not** flowers! It is **not** something to eat! It's something much more fun. Shall I tell you?

I'm growing birdhouses.
Really I am!

I started last year. I put seeds in jars. I waited a long time. Suddenly, little green plants came up. I could hardly see them. But they were there!

Pretty soon, my plants got much too big for the jars. So I had to dig a hole for them.

Digging was hard work! But you know what? It wasn't nearly as hard as waiting!

I could hardly stand it!
I wish, wish, wish birdhouses didn't
grow so slowly!

After a long time, they got big.
They got yellow flowers. Then the
stems near the flowers got dark
green and started to swell. I knew
those parts would be birdhouses!
They got big and fat like these.

See? I really did grow birdhouses! I picked them and let them dry. Then my dad got to work. He cut holes for the birds to go in and out.

I got out my art stuff. I painted them. It was fun!

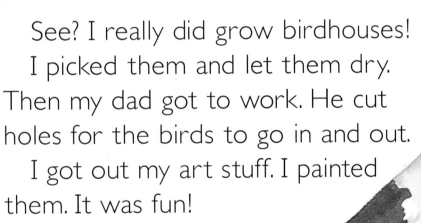

One large plant had a lot of seeds. I gave the seeds to my friends to plant.

Now just look at these! All that work really paid off!

Soon all our yards will be filled
with birds. Bluebirds! That's what I
want. I can hardly wait.

The Garden

by Arnold Lobel

Frog was in his garden.
Toad came walking by.
"What a fine garden
you have, Frog," he said.

"Yes," said Frog. "It is very
nice, but it was hard work."

"I wish I had a garden,"
said Toad.

"Here are some flower seeds.
Plant them in the ground," said
Frog, "and soon you will have
a garden."

"How soon?" asked Toad.

"Quite soon," said Frog.

Toad ran home.

He planted the flower seeds.

"Now seeds," said Toad,

"start growing."

Toad walked up and down
a few times.

The seeds did not start to grow.

Toad put his head close to the
ground and said loudly,
"Now seeds, start growing!"

Toad looked at the ground again.
The seeds did not start to grow.

Toad put his head very
close to the ground and shouted,
"NOW SEEDS, START GROWING!"

Frog came running up the path.
"What is all this noise?" he asked.

"My seeds will not grow," said Toad.

"You are shouting too much,"
said Frog. "These poor seeds
are afraid to grow."

"My seeds are afraid to grow?"
asked Toad.

"Of course," said Frog.

"Leave them alone for a few days.

Let the sun shine on them,

let the rain fall on them.

Soon your seeds will start to grow."

That night Toad looked out
of his window.
"Drat!" said Toad.
"My seeds have not started to
grow. They must be afraid of
the dark."

Toad went out to his garden
with some candles.
"I will read the seeds a story,"
said Toad. "Then they will
not be afraid."

Toad read a long story
to his seeds.

All the next day
Toad sang songs
to his seeds.

And all the next day
Toad read poems
to his seeds.

And all the next day
Toad played music
for his seeds.

Toad looked at the ground.
The seeds still did not
start to grow.
"What shall I do?" cried Toad.
"These must be the most
frightened seeds in the
whole world!"

Then Toad felt very tired,
and he fell asleep.

"Toad, Toad, wake up," said Frog.
"Look at your garden!"

Toad looked at his garden.
Little green plants were coming
up out of the ground.

"At last," shouted Toad,
"my seeds have stopped
being afraid to grow!"

"And now you will have
a nice garden too," said Frog.

"Yes," said Toad,
"but you were right, Frog.
It was very hard work."

About the Author and Illustrator

Arnold Lobel

"There is a little world at the end of my pencil," said Arnold Lobel about writing books. He wrote almost one hundred books. His Frog and Toad books are the most well known.

Mr. Lobel watched his children catch frogs and toads. That gave him ideas for the Frog and Toad stories.

Field Row
by Alma Flor Ada

In the field row
lies a seed, all tucked in
like a baby in the crib.
Sleep tight today, seed.
Wake up tomorrow, plant.

Surco
por Alma Flor Ada

En el surco
la semilla arropada
como el niñito en la cuna.
Duérmete, semilla, hoy.
Despierta, planta, mañana.

Reader Response

Let's Talk

Toad sang songs and read poems to his seeds. What would you do to help seeds grow?

Write a Song, Poem, or Cheer

1. Write a song, poem, or cheer to Toad's seeds.
2. Sing it or read it to your class.

Language Arts

Growing Things

A **sentence** tells a complete idea.

It has a naming part and an action part.

A sentence begins with a capital letter.

A question ends with a **?**.

What does Paul grow in his garden**?**

A telling sentence ends with a **.**.

Paul grows flowers and strawberries**.**

Talk

What would you grow in a garden?

Answer in a sentence.

Write

Write about what you would grow in a garden.

Check your sentences.

How can you make them better?

Jordan Makes a New Friend

by David A. Adler

illustrated by C. D. Hullinger

Jordan looked outside. Snow was coming down. Wind was blowing the snow off the walk into large drifts.

"Mark called," Jordan's mother said. "He can't get here in the storm."

Jordan said, "But Mark
told me he would come.
I like playing with him.
We play games. He likes
my stories. He's good at
sharing."

When the snow stopped falling and
the wind stopped blowing, Jordan
went outside. He made a snow fort
and a snowman. He named the
snowman Mort.

He gave Mort an old scarf so Mort
would not get cold.

Jordan and Mort played Hide and Seek. Jordan found Mort every time, but Mort never found Jordan.

Jordan told Mort a story.
Mort liked it. Jordan made
two snowcones. One for
him and one for Mort.
    Mort let Jordan have his.

Jordan's mother said, "Come inside. It's cold. Your coat and hat are full of snow."

Before Jordan went in, he said to Mort,
"We played games. You liked my story.
You are good at sharing, just like Mark."
"I am?" someone said.
Jordan jumped. "Mort, you can talk!"

"It's me," Mark said. He stepped
out from behind Mort. "The snowstorm
stopped, so here I am."

"I'm glad you came," Jordan said
as they went inside. "Playing with
Mort was fun. Playing with you will
be even better."

Ice-Cold Birthday

by Maryann Cocca-Leffler

Some people have all the luck!
I have luck too.
Bad luck.
The week before the dance show,
I broke my arm.

The year I held
the flag in the
parade, it rained.

And the day of
our class pictures,
I spilled green
paint all over my
new dress.
But on my birthday
I was sure my luck
would change.

My birthday
started out great.
It was snowing!
Everything looked
so pretty.

Dad made a
birthday pancake.
It was a seven.

At school I got an A in math.
But the best part was still to come.
Six friends were coming to my party.

After school I ran home.
The snow was coming down hard.
And it was very windy.

Mom was baking a big cake.
Dad was blowing up balloons.
My sister set the table with
party plates and candy.
What a great party this was
going to be.

49

Then I heard the radio . . . .

~BAD STORM IS HERE~
~TWO FEET OF SNOW~
~HIGH WINDS~

"Oh no! My party!" I said.

"Don't worry," said Dad.
"With luck the storm will pass."

Luck? I have no luck!

That's when it happened.
The radio stopped playing.
The cake stopped baking.
All the lights went off.
The power was out.
Then the calls came.
No one could come
to my party.

"I knew it!
I knew it!"
I cried.

I put on my coat.
I sat down and
stared at the
blank TV.
No cake.
No party.
No fun.
Just an ice-cold
birthday!

Then Mom came in.
She had a funny cake.
It was made of ice cream
and cookies.
I had to smile.
I made a wish and blew
out the candles.

We ate my cake.
Then Dad held the flashlight.
We made shadow puppets.

Later, everybody played pin-the-tail-on-the-donkey.
It was so dark.
Nobody needed blindfolds.

Then Mom told
a spooky story.
It was about
Iceman.
I had to admit it.
I was having fun.

The best part was when
Mom and Dad brought
in my big surprise.
It was a brand-new sled!
It had stopped snowing.
So we all went sledding.

The moon was full.
And snow, snow, snow
was everywhere.
Up and down the hill we went.
When it got too cold,
we started back home.

We got to the front yard.
"Look!" said Dad.
He wrote "Happy Birthday"
in the snow.
"That's the biggest card
you will ever get!"

"Lucky for me, it snowed!" I said.
Then I heard my words.
Maybe I don't have such bad luck
after all.

About the Author and Illustrator

Maryann Cocca-Leffler

Many of Maryann Cocca-Leffler's books tell stories of things that really happened. "The idea for the ice-cream cookie cake in *Ice-Cold Birthday* came from a cake we made for my sister when we forgot her birthday," says Ms. Cocca-Leffler.

Ms. Cocca-Leffler dedicated her book to her sister. She wrote, "For my sister Diane, may you never go without a real birthday cake again!"

Sunflakes

by Frank Asch

If sunlight fell like snowflakes,
gleaming yellow and so bright,
we could build a sunman,
we could have a sunball fight,
we could watch the sunflakes
drifting in the sky.

We could go sleighing

in the middle of July

through sundrifts and sunbanks,

we could ride a sunmobile,

and we could touch sunflakes—

I wonder how they'd feel.

Let's Talk

The girl's family turned a bad day into a good day. What did you like best about the girl's birthday? Why?

Stormy Day List

The girl thought the storm had spoiled her fun. What can you do for fun on a stormy day? Make a list of things you can do.

Stormy Day List
Make cookies.
Build with blocks.
Put on a play.
Draw pictu

What a Day!

An **exclamation** is a sentence
that shows strong feelings.
An exclamation begins with
a capital letter.
It ends with an **!**.

I wish this rain would stop!

What a great book!

Talk

Name a book you like.
Tell why you like the book.
Use an exclamation.

Write

Write a report about
a book you like. Try to
use an exclamation in
your report.

Show Time
Your First Play
by Phyllis Root

What do you need to put on a play?
First, you need a play. You can find
one in a book. Or you can make one
up. Once you have a play, everyone
needs to work together.

Who will play the parts? Some actors may be taller. Other actors may be smaller. Who will be best for each part? Which person or animal do you want to play?

You may need to make costumes.
Ask a grown-up for things you can use.
A fur coat turns you into a bear. A big
red shirt turns you into a bird.

You can make props too. Boxes make good props. You can even paint the boxes. A smaller box can be a chair. A bigger box can be a table. The biggest box can be a bed.

Now you need to learn your part.
First say your lines over and over. Say
them to each other. Do you need to
speak faster or slower?

Who will come to your play? Ask
your family. Ask your friends. Put up
posters that say SEE THE BIGGEST SHOW
UNDER THE SUN.

At last it's time for your play. Once the play starts, don't stop. You can help each other out if someone forgets a line. The show must go on!

When the play is over, say "Thank
you" when people clap. Your play will
be the best! Have a party after the
play. Then plan another big show.

Do You Live in a Nest?

by Carmen Tafolla

illustrated by Lee Lee Brazeal

CHARACTERS

CRICKET

FROG

DOG

TURTLE

HORSE

BIRD

LION

FROG: Hi, Cricket!

CRICKET: Frog! Frog! Bird is coming to visit.

FROG: I am happy to hear that. Bird makes the sweetest sounds.

CRICKET: Where will she stay?

FROG: She can stay with me!

CRICKET: Do you live in a nest?

FROG: No, I live in a nice, wet pond. There are lots of flies to eat! Once Bird is here, she can pick which fly she wants.

CRICKET: I do not think Bird wants a pond. She needs some place warmer than that.

TURTLE: Hi, Cricket! Hi, Frog!

CRICKET: Turtle! Turtle! Bird is coming to visit!

TURTLE: I am happy to hear that. Bird makes the sweetest sounds.

CRICKET: Where will she stay?

TURTLE: She can stay with me!

CRICKET: Do you live in a nest?

TURTLE: No, I live in a flat field near the pond. It has nice, green grass! Once Bird is here, she can eat all the grass she wants.

CRICKET: I do not think Bird wants a field. She needs some place rounder than that.

DOG: Hi, Cricket! Hi, Frog! Hi, Turtle!

CRICKET: Dog! Dog! Bird is coming to visit!

DOG: I am happy to hear that. Bird makes the sweetest sounds.

CRICKET: Where will she stay?

DOG: She can stay with me!

CRICKET: Do you live in a nest?

DOG: No, I sleep on the ground under a big tree. There are lots of bones hidden under the tree! Once Bird is here, she can pick which bone she wants.

CRICKET: I do not think Bird wants to sleep on the ground. She needs some place higher than that.

86

HORSE: Hi, Cricket! Hi, Frog! Hi, Turtle! Hi, Dog!

CRICKET: Horse! Horse! Bird is coming to visit!

HORSE: I am happy to hear that. Bird makes the sweetest sounds.

CRICKET: Where will she stay?

HORSE: She can stay with me!

CRICKET: Do you live in a nest?

HORSE: No, I live in a nice big barn. There are many bundles of hay! Once Bird is here, she can pick any bundle she wants.

CRICKET: I do not think Bird wants a barn. She needs some place smaller than that.

LION: Roar!

CRICKET: Lion! Bird is coming to visit.

LION: I am happy to hear that. Bird makes the sweetest sounds.

CRICKET: Where will she stay?

LION: I am the king. I do not like other animals in my way, but Bird is a visitor. She can stay with me!

CRICKET: Do you live in a nest?

LION: No, I live on a great big rock. There are lots of rabbits around to chase! Once Bird is here, she can pick which rabbit she wants.

CRICKET: I do not think Bird wants a rock. She needs some place softer than that.

LION: You're right. Bird needs some place softer.

HORSE: She needs some place smaller.

DOG: She needs some place higher.

TURTLE: She needs some place rounder.

FROG: She needs some place warmer.

CRICKET: Bird needs a nest!

LION: Horse, what are you doing?

HORSE: I am getting some hay. We are going to build a nest for her.

TURTLE: Thank you for the hay, Horse. But how can we make a nest?

DOG: I can roll the hay and make it round.
I love to play with a ball.

FROG: Turtle, what are you doing?

TURTLE: I can pat a warm place in the hay
for Bird.

DOG: Thank you, Turtle. It is a great nest.

LION: Where do we put it?

CRICKET: I know where we can find the tallest tree!

LION: How do we get it up in the tree?

FROG: Lion, pick it up with your claws. Put it on my back. I will jump up into the tree. I will put Bird's nest on the highest branch.

BIRD: Cricket! Cricket! I've come to visit!

CRICKET: We have a nest for you! Do you like it?

BIRD: Oh, it's the softest, smallest, highest, roundest, warmest nest of all! Which one of you made the nest?

HORSE: We all helped each other. Now we can help each other do one more thing.

ALL: Yes! Let's have a party!

The First Grade's Play

Mrs. Cruz's class put on the play *Do You Live in a Nest?* The children sold tickets. They made this chart to show how many tickets they sold each day.

Tickets Sold by First Graders	Kerri	Luis	Sidra	Adam
Monday	I \	/\ I·I		I \
Tuesday	I	/\ /		I \ I
Wednesday	/\		I \	
Thursday	I		/\ \	
Friday	I \	/I	/I	I\ /\

Let's Talk

Who sold tickets every day?
On which day did the children sell the most tickets?

About the Author

Carmen Tafolla

When Carmen Tafolla was a little girl, her Aunt Esther told her a bedtime story about an ant. That story gave Dr. Tafolla the idea for *Do You Live in a Nest?* Dr. Tafolla wrote her play about a cricket, not an ant. But one thing she kept the same. The animals in both work together to make everyone happy.

Reader Response

Readers Theater

What you need:

name tags

What you do:

1. Work in groups of seven children.
2. Pick who will read the parts of Frog, Cricket, Turtle, Dog, Horse, Lion, and Bird.
3. Read and act out the play.

Let's Talk

Which animal in the play was most helpful? Why?

Act It Out

A **command** is a sentence that tells someone to do something. A command begins with a capital letter. It ends with a .

Pick up the nest. Put it on my back.

Lion

Frog

Talk

Tell someone directions for making the nest in *Do You Live in a Nest?* Tell the steps in order. Use words such as *first, next, then,* and *last.*

Write

What do you have to do to put on a play? Write the steps in order. Use words such as *first, next, then,* and *last.*

What's New in Mrs. Powell's Class?

by Anne Sibley O'Brien
illustrated by Gil Ashby

"It's newsletter time," Mrs. Powell told
her class. "What can we tell parents about?"
"The trip to the farm," said Jason.
"And don't forget about the cows
running away!" said Danny.

"Good idea," said Mrs. Powell.
"What else?"

"The play," said Lola, "so lots
of people will come see us."

"Great!" said Mrs. Powell. "Now
let's get to work."

Mrs. Powell's Class News

Mr. Brown's Farm

We went on a field trip to see Mr. Brown's cows. Mariko forgot to pull the gate shut. All the cows got out. Mr. Brown had to chase them down the road and along the river.

We want to thank Mr. Brown and his
cows for a great time. Danny said
it really was a field trip because
the cows were in the field. Ha ha.

A Funny Play

Please come to our class play on Monday at 2:00. It tells how a jester saves a town from a dragon. He goes to the dragon and tells riddles. The dragon likes the riddles better than scaring people.

Lola is the queen. She wears a crown and a fancy gown.

Jason is a scary dragon. He prowls along the wall.

Danny likes to be funny so he is the jester. This play will make you howl.

Fox on Stage

by James Marshall

One Saturday morning
Fox and his friends were
just lying around.

"What a sad little group,"
said Mom.
"Why don't you *do* something?"

"The television is broken,"
said Fox.

"Oh, that *is* terrible!"
said Mom.

Then Fox had one of his
great ideas.

"Let's put on a play!" he said.
"We can charge everyone a dime."

"We'll get rich!" said Dexter.

"I'll buy a new car," said Carmen.

And they went to the library.

"Let's do a spooky play," said Carmen.
"We can scare all the little kids."

"Here's what you need," said Miss Pencil.
"It's called *Spooky Plays.*
My favorite is 'The Mummy's Toe.' "

"Oooh," said the gang.

Fox and the gang went home to practice.

"The Mummy's Toe" was *very* scary.

Dexter played the mummy.

Carmen was the princess.

And Fox was the hero.

Soon things were moving right along.

Fox and Dexter worked hard

on the set.

And Carmen put up posters

all over town.

Mom and Louise helped out
with the costumes.

"Hold still," said Mom.

"I hope I'm scary enough," said Dexter.
It was time for the play.

Fox peeked out from behind the curtain.
There was a big crowd.

"I hope everything goes okay,"
said Dexter.

"What could go wrong?" said Fox.

The curtain went up.

And the play began.

Right away Carmen forgot her lines.

"Well, I *did* know them," she said to the audience.

Then Dexter crashed through
the scenery.
"Whoops," said Dexter.

It was Fox's turn to appear.

Suddenly it began to rain.

Fox's beautiful paper costume

fell apart in front of everyone.

"What do we do now?" said Carmen.

"Pull the curtain down!"

Fox called out to Louise.

And Louise pulled with all her might.

The curtain came down.

"Who turned out the lights?"
cried Carmen.

"Where am I?" said Dexter.

"The play is ruined!" cried Fox.
"*Everything* went wrong!"

The next day Fox heard
some folks talking.

"That Fox really knows how to put on a funny show," someone said.

"Funniest thing I ever saw," said someone else.

And Fox began to plan his next show.

About the Author and Illustrator

James Marshall wrote many books about friendship. He added drawings to show friends together. Mr. Marshall wrote eleven books about Fox and his friends.

"You have to make a book *move,*" Mr. Marshall said about writing. "There always has to be a reason to turn to the next page." He always tried to add a really special ending. Does "Fox on Stage" have one of those endings?

Let's Talk

There is a mummy, a princess, and a hero in Fox's play. Which part would you want to play? Why?

Fox and the Gang present

The First Day starts at 7:00

Make a Poster

Carmen needs your help. She wants to make a poster for Fox's next play. Make it for her.

You and I

A **pronoun** is a word that can take the place of a noun. These words are pronouns.

**I   we   you   he
she   it   they**

Jan wants to jump rope.
She wants to jump rope.
<u>She</u> takes the place of <u>Jan</u> in this sentence.

Talk

What game do you like to play? How could you get others to play it with you?

Write

Write an ad for a game you like. What can you say to make others try it?

123

Doggy Art

by David McPhail

One day Jill painted a picture.
Then she went outside to play.
    She left her paints on the living
room floor.

Along came Jill's dog, Rudy.
Rudy sat down beside the paints.
His tail was in the paint. Rudy
wagged his tail. His tail painted a
picture.

Rudy thought painting was fun. Rudy painted another picture. There was no more paper so he painted on the rug.

Rudy kept painting. He painted a flower on a chair.

After that, he painted a tree and
some clouds on the sofa. When Jill's
mother came home, Rudy went out.
Jill's mother went into the living room.
What she found almost made her shout.

Jill came in. "Do you like my painting?" she asked her mother.

"Did you paint the rug?" asked Jill's mother. "And the sofa and the chair?"

"No," Jill said, "just this picture."

Jill's mother went to the door.
"Rudy!" she called.

Rudy came into the house. Rudy
was covered with paint.

"Now I know who painted the
rug and the chair and the sofa,"
Jill's mother said.

"Maybe Rudy thinks he is an
artist," said Jill.

"Maybe," thought Jill's mother,
and she laughed. Jill laughed too.

Then she helped her mother
clean the living room. Jill knew Rudy
needed cleaning too. So after that,
Rudy took a bath.

The Snow Glory

by Cynthia Rylant
illustrated by Suçie Stevenson

When the snow melted
and spring came,
Henry and his dog Mudge
stayed outside
all the time.

Henry had missed
riding his bike.
Mudge had missed
chewing on sticks.
They were glad
it was warmer.

One day when Henry and Mudge

were in their yard,

Henry saw something blue

on the ground.

He got closer to it.

"Mudge!" he called.

"It's a flower!"

Mudge slowly walked over

and sniffed the blue flower.

Then he sneezed

all over Henry.

"Aw, Mudge," Henry said.

Later, Henry's mother
told him that the flower
was called a snow glory.

"Can I pick it?"
Henry asked.

"Oh, no," said his mother.
"Let it grow."

So Henry didn't pick it.

Every day he saw the snow glory

in the yard,

blue

and looking so pretty.

He knew he shouldn't pick it.

He was trying not to pick it.

But he thought how nice

it would look in a jar.

He thought how nice

to bring it inside.

He thought how nice

it would be

to own that snow glory.

Every day he stood with Mudge

and looked at the flower.

Mudge would stick his nose

into the grass

all around the snow glory.

But he never looked at it

the way Henry did.

"Don't you think the snow glory

has been growing long enough?"

Henry would ask his mother.

"Let it grow, Henry,"

she would say.

Oh, Henry wanted that snow glory.

And one day

he just knew

he had to have it.

So he took Mudge

by the collar

and he stood

beside the snow glory.

"I'm going to pick it,"

Henry whispered to Mudge.

"I've let it grow a long time."

Henry bent his head and

he said in Mudge's ear,

"Now I *need* it."

And Mudge wagged his tail,

licked Henry's face,

then put his big mouth

right over that snow glory . . .

and he ate it.

"*No, Mudge!*" Henry said.

But too late.
There was a blue flower
in Mudge's belly.

"I said *need* it, not *eat* it!"

shouted Henry.

He was so mad because

Mudge took his flower.

It was Henry's flower

and Mudge took it.

And Henry almost said,
"Bad dog," but he stopped.
He looked at Mudge,
who looked back at him
with soft brown eyes
and a flower in his belly.

Henry knew it wasn't his snow glory.

He knew it wasn't anybody's snow glory.

Just a thing to let grow.

And if someone ate it,

it was just a thing to let go.

Henry stopped feeling mad.

He put his arms around

Mudge's big head.

"Next time, Mudge,"

he said,

"try to *listen* better."

Mudge wagged his tail

and licked his lips.

One blue petal

fell from his mouth

into Henry's hand.

Henry smiled,

put it in his pocket,

and they went inside.

About the Author

Cynthia Rylant once worked as a children's librarian. After reading children's books, she knew that she wanted to write for children.

Caring for her son, Nate, and two dogs gave her the idea for her Henry and Mudge stories. "I know about cold shivers, big tests, happy cats, and wild winds," she says. "And especially big drooly lovable dogs."

About the Illustrator

Suçie Stevenson has done all the drawings for the Henry and Mudge books. She has also written her own books.

Ms. Stevenson lives with two dogs too. Sometimes her dogs are right under her desk while she works. "If I ever forget how Mudge would act, I just look under my desk," she says.

Let's Talk

If you were Henry, would you be mad at Mudge? Why or why not?

Make a Paper Flower

What you need:

soft paper

small wire

What you do:

1

Fold three sheets of soft paper in half.

2

Wrap a small wire around the soft paper.

3

Unfold the paper.

4

Use the flower to tell the story of Henry and Mudge.

150

He Was Surprised!

Pronouns take the place of nouns. Use these pronouns in the naming part of a sentence.

I   he   she   we   they

Use these pronouns in the action part of a sentence.

me   him   her   us   them

Mother told **Henry** to let the flower grow.
She told **him** to let the flower grow.
She takes the place of Mother.
Him takes the place of Henry.

Talk

Tell about the pictures on pages 142 and 143.
Tell what is happening.
What surprised Henry?

Write

Pick a picture in one of your stories.
Write about it.
Tell what is happening.

I'll Join You

by Juanita Havill
illustrated by Michele Noiset

"My dad says we might move,"
said Erin.
"Where will you go?" said Moy.
"Dad didn't say," said Erin.
"You are my best friend," said
Moy. "Somehow I'll join you."

"What if I move downtown? Then I'll go to another school," said Erin.

"I'll open my piggy bank. I'll grab some coins to pay for the bus," said Moy. "I'll ride downtown and join you at your new school."

"What if I move across the river?" said Erin.

"I'll pack my suitcase with toys and go across in a big boat. I'll enjoy the ride to the other side," said Moy. "We'll always be friends."

"What if I move across the mountains?" said Erin.

"I'll go up the slope. Then I'll ski downhill to the other side," said Moy. "We'll always be friends."

"What if I move across the sea to China?" said Erin.

"I'll become a pilot. I'll fly my airplane to China," said Moy. "We'll always be friends."

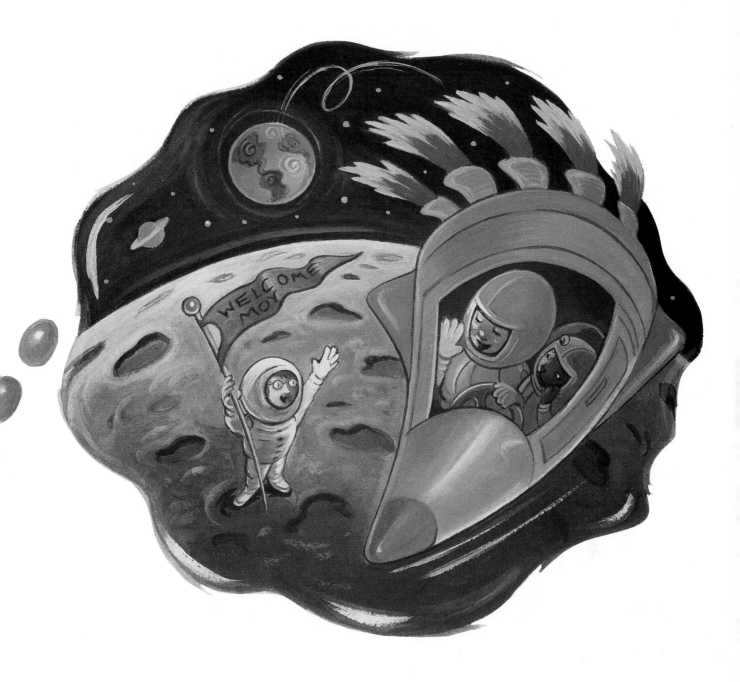

"What if I move to the moon?"
said Erin.

"I'll become an astronaut. I'll fly
to the moon in my spaceship," said
Moy. "We'll always be friends."

"Hi, girls!" Erin's dad said. "Did Erin tell you we are moving, Moy?"

"Yes," said Moy. "I'll join her wherever she goes—downtown, across the river, over the mountains, across the sea, or to the moon."

"You won't have to go so far,"
said Erin's dad. "We are moving to
the townhouse across the street."
Erin opened her eyes wide.
Moy said, "Oh, boy!"
Both girls shouted for joy, "Yes!"

LEON and BOB

by Simon James

Leon had moved into town
with his mom.
His dad was away in the army.
Leon shared his room
with his new friend, Bob.

No one else could see Bob,

but Leon knew he was there.

Leon always laid a place

for Bob at the table.

"More milk, Bob?" Leon said.

Sometimes Leon's mom

couldn't take Leon to school,

but Leon didn't mind.

He always walked to school with Bob.

He always had Bob to talk to.

Often, when Leon got home,

there was a letter waiting for him

from his dad.

Bob liked to hear Leon read it

over and over again.

One Saturday, Leon heard

some noises in the street below.

He saw a new family moving in next door.

A boy looked up at Leon and waved.

Leon waved back.

That night Leon kept thinking
about the boy next door.
He decided to go by there
in the morning.
"But you'll have to come with
me, Bob," he said.

The next day Leon and Bob
ate their breakfast
very quickly.
Then Leon grabbed his ball
and rushed outside.

Leon ran up the steps
of the house next door.
He was about halfway
when suddenly he realized
Bob wasn't there anymore.

Leon sat down.

He was all alone.

He could ring the bell

or he could go home.

Why wasn't Bob there

to help him?

Leon rang the bell and waited.

The door opened.

"Hello," said the boy.

"H-hello," said Leon.

"Would you like to go to the park?"

"Okay," said the boy.

"I'm just going to the park, Mom,"
he called.

Together Leon and the boy walked
down the steps toward the street.

"My name's Leon," said Leon.
"What's yours?"

"Bob," said Bob.

About the Author and Illustrator

Simon James lives in England where he writes books and teaches art to children. Mr. James had fourteen jobs before he went to art school and became an author.

He says that he wants the idea for a book to come to him "on its own."

Making Friends

by Eloise Greenfield

when I was in kindergarten
this new girl came in our class one day
and the teacher told her to sit beside me
and I didn't know what to say
so I wiggled my nose and made my bunny face

and she laughed
then she puffed out her cheeks
and she made a funny face
and I laughed
so then
we were friends

Reader Response

Let's Talk

Leon walked to school with Bob. What would you want to do with Bob?

Tell About a New Friend

Make up a new best friend. Tell all about that friend. Draw the new friend and give him or her a name.

Opal

Boxes of Fun

A noun can mean one or more than one.

Add **-s** or **-es** to mean more than one.

Add **-es** to nouns that end in **x, s, ch,** or **sh**.

We can play with the moving **boxes**.

We can pretend they are **buses**.

Talk

The girl in the picture is inviting a friend. Tell what you think the girl is saying. What do you say when you invite a friend?

Write

Write a letter to ask a friend to visit. What can you say to make your friend want to come?

Words from Your Stories

Aa

actors Actors are people who act in a play or in movies and television.

actors

admit To **admit** something is to say that it is true. She **admitted** that I was right.

appear To **appear** means to come in sight. Stars **appear** in the sky at night.

army An **army** is a large group of soldiers.

Bb

beautiful **Beautiful** means that something we see or hear is very pretty. That was a **beautiful** song.

behind **Behind** means in back of. The band marched **behind** the leader.

behind

birds   Birds have feathers, wings, and two legs. Most **birds** can fly.

blindfolds   Blindfolds are pieces of cloth that cover the eyes. The players in the game all wore **blindfolds**.

brought   If you **brought** something, you carried it with you. We **brought** presents to the party.

brought

bundles   Bundles are things tied up together. We carried **bundles** of newspapers.

Cc ───────────────────────────

candles   Candles are sticks of wax with a string in their center. **Candles** give light as they burn.

change   Change means to become different. Leaves **change** color in the fall.

charge   To **charge** means to ask as a price. The store **charges** two dollars for milk.

charge

closer Closer means nearer. If you move the book **closer** to me, I can read along.

costumes Costumes are clothes that you can put on to look like someone else. **Costumes** are worn in plays or just for fun.

costumes

cricket A **cricket** is an insect. The male **cricket** makes a loud noise by rubbing its front wings together.

Dd

decided If you have **decided**, you have chosen or made up your mind. Kim **decided** to eat the apple, not the cookie.

Ee

enough There is **enough** food for everyone. Have you eaten **enough?**

eyes The **eyes** are the parts of the body that help you see. Your **eyes** are in your face.

Ff

flowers Flowers are parts of plants. Roses and tulips are **flowers.**

folks Folks is another word for people.

flowers

frightened   If you are **frightened**, you are scared or afraid. Al's cat was **frightened** by the dog mask.

frightened

Gg

great   **Great** means very big or large. A **great** cloud of smoke rose over the fire.

ground   **Ground** means the soil or dirt on the Earth. We planted seeds in the **ground**.

group   A **group** is a number of persons or things together. One **group** of children played ball, and another **group** jumped rope.

Jj

jester   A **jester** is a person who makes jokes. Long ago, kings and queens often had **jesters** to make them laugh.

Ll

listen   **Listen** means to hear or try to hear. Most people like to **listen** to music.

loudly   **Loudly** means done in a noisy way. The dog barked **loudly**.

loudly

Mm

moving   If you are **moving**, you are going from one place to another. If something is **moving** along, it is getting better.

music   The sounds made by a piano, a violin, and other instruments are **music**. The sound of a person singing is also **music**.

Nn

noise   **Noise** means a sound we do not want to hear. Loud **noise** can wake you up.

noise

Oo

of course   **Of course** means surely or certainly. **Of course** you will learn to read well.

often   If something happens **often**, it happens many times. We **often** go to the movies together.

often

Pp

poems   **Poems** are a kind of writing that is something like songs without any music. **Poems** often use rhyme.

posters   **Posters** are large printed pieces of paper put up for everyone to see.

power Power is energy that can do work. Running water can produce electric **power.**

props Props are things used in a play, movie, or TV show.

Qq

quite Quite can mean very. It is **quite** cold today. Dinner will be ready **quite** soon.

Rr

realized If you **realized** something, you understood it clearly. We **realized** that she did a good job.

ruined When something is **ruined**, it is spoiled completely. The bicycle was **ruined** in the accident.

ruined

Ss

scary Scary means making someone feel afraid. He saw a **scary** movie.

shared If you **shared** something, you used it with someone else. The twins **shared** a bedroom.

sharing My brother and I are good at **sharing.**

sharing

shouldn't   **Shouldn't** means should not.

snow glory   A **snow glory** is a kind of flower.

stared   If you **stared** at something, you looked at it with your eyes wide open for a long time.

stood   If you **stood**, you were on your feet instead of sitting down. We **stood** in line for tickets.

stood

surprise   Something that happens that you did not plan is a **surprise.**

Tt

television   When you turn on a **television**, you can see pictures and hear sounds. You can watch shows on **television.**

toward   **Toward** means in the direction of. I walked **toward** home.

toward

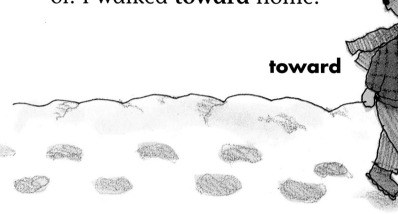

Vv

visitor A **visitor** is someone who goes to see places or people. The **visitors** from Italy asked us how to get to the hotel.

Ww

warmer **Warmer** means more warm than something else. Summer is **warmer** than winter.

wherever Please sit **wherever** you like. **Wherever** you want to go is fine with me.

whispered If you **whispered**, you spoke very softly and low. I couldn't hear him when he **whispered.**

would **Would** you like some candy? She said she **would** come to visit me.

wrong **Wrong** means not right or not true. She gave the **wrong** answer.

wrote The teacher **wrote** on the board. I **wrote** a poem about winter.

Tested Word List

Bluebirds in the Garden
The Garden

ground
much
shall
these
wish
work

Jordan Makes a New Friend
Ice-Cold Birthday

before
cold
full
off
would

Show Time: Your First Play
Do You Live in a Nest?

each
once
other
under
which

What's New in Mrs. Powell's Class?
Fox on Stage

along
goes
great
idea
pull

Doggy Art
The Snow Glory

almost
knew
picture
thought
took

I'll Join You
Leon and Bob

always
boy
move
open
school

Acknowledgments

Text
Page 18: "The Garden" from *Frog and Toad Together* by Arnold Lobel, pp. 18–29. Copyright © 1971, 1972 by Arnold Lobel. Reprinted by permission of HarperCollins Publishers, Inc.
Page 31: "Surco/Field Row" from *Gathering the Sun* by Alma Flor Ada, English translation by Rosa Zubizarreta. Text copyright © 1997 by Alma Flor Ada. Reprinted by permission of Lothrop, Lee & Shepard Books, a division of William Morrow & Company, Inc.
Page 42: *Ice-Cold Birthday* by Maryann Cocca-Leffler, pp. 4–32. Copyright © 1992 by Maryann Cocca-Leffler. Reprinted by permission of Grosset & Dunlap, Inc., a division of Penguin Putnam, Inc.
Page 68: "Sunflakes" from *Country Pie* by Frank Asch. Copyright © 1979 by Frank Asch. Reprinted by permission of Greenwillow Books, a division of William Morrow & Company, Inc.
Page 106: "Fox on Stage" from *Fox on Stage* by James Marshall, pp. 34–48. Copyright © 1993 by the Estate of James Marshall. Reprinted by permission of Dial Books for Young Readers, a division of Penguin Putnam, Inc.
Page 124: © 1998 David McPhail
Page 134: "The Snow Glory" from *Henry and Mudge in Puddle Trouble* by Cynthia Rylant, pictures by Suçie Stevenson, pp. 4–19. Text copyright © 1987 by Cynthia Rylant. Illustrations copyright © 1987 by Suçie Stevenson. Reprinted by permission of Simon & Schuster Books for Young Readers, Simon &

Schuster Children's Publishing Division.
Page 165: *Leon and Bob* by Simon James. Copyright © 1997 by Simon James. Reprinted by permission of Candlewick Press, Inc., Cambridge, MA.
Page 183: "Making Friends" from *Nathaniel Talking* by Eloise Greenfield. Copyright © 1998 by Eloise Greenfield. Reprinted by permission of Scott Treimel New York.

Artists
Maryjane Begin, cover, 8–9
Eliza Schulte Holliday, (calligraphy) 9
Meg Aubrey, 10–17
Arnold Lobel, 18–30
Glen T. Strock, 31
Mary Collier, 32–33
C. D. Hullinger, 34–41
Maryann Cocca-Leffler, 42–67
Susan Spellman, 68–69
Anne Kennedy, 70–71
Lee Lee Brazeal, 80–97
Anthony Lewis, 98–99
Gil Ashby, 100–105
James Marshall, 106–121
Clive Scruton, 122–123
David McPhail, 124–131
Suçie Stevenson, 132–148
Pamela Paulsrud, (calligraphy) 132
Kristin Kest, 151
Michele Noiset, 152–159

Simon James, 160–180
Jan Spivey Gilchrist, 181
Stephen Lewis, 183

Photographs
Page 7 Richard Hutchings for Scott Foresman
Page 10 Courtesy of the family, Photo: Lifetouch
Pages 13, 15, 17 Courtesy of the family
Page 30 Courtesy HarperCollins Publishers/Photo: Ian Anderson
Page 67 Richard Hutchings for Scott Foresman
Page 97 Jim Markham for Scott Foresman
Page 148 © Carlo Ontal from *Best Wishes* by Cynthia Rylant, courtesy of Richard C. Owen Publishers, Inc., Katonah, NY
Page 149 Courtesy Suçie Stevenson
Page 180 Courtesy Candlewick Press
Page 186 PhotoDisc, Inc.

Glossary
The contents of this glossary have been adapted from *My First Picture Dictionary*, Revised Edition, Copyright © 1990 by Scott, Foresman and Company, or from *My Second Picture Dictionary*, Revised Edition, Copyright © 1990 by Scott, Foresman and Company.